border to border · teen to teen · border to border · teen to teen · border to border

Teens in NEPAL

by Nicki Yackley-Franken

Content Adviser: Mark Turin, Ph.D.,
Director, Digital Himalaya Project,
Department of Social Anthropology,
University of Cambridge, U.K.

Reading Adviser: Alexa L. Sandmann, Ph.D.,
Professor of Literacy,
Kent State University

Compass Point Books ◈ Minneapolis, Minnesota

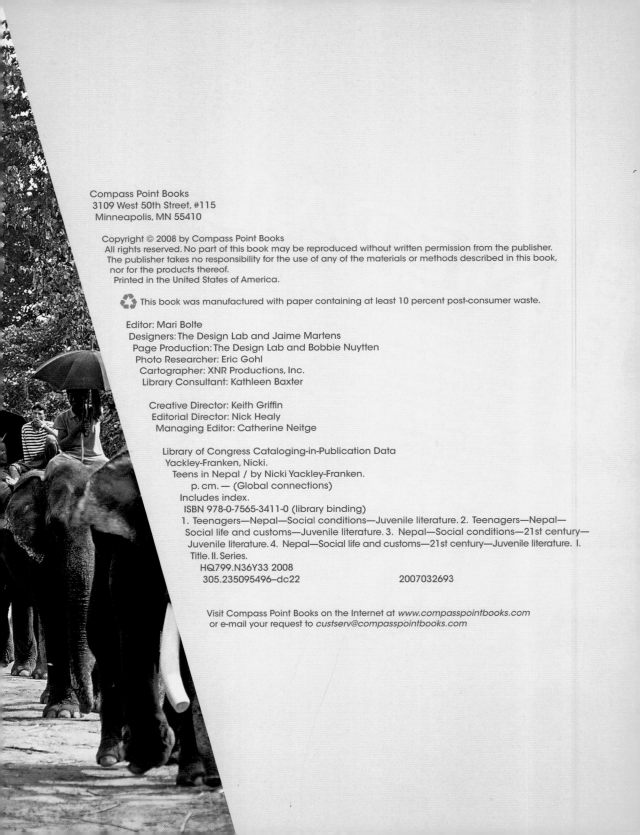

Compass Point Books
3109 West 50th Street, #115
Minneapolis, MN 55410

This book was manufactured with paper containing at least 10 percent post-consumer waste.

Editor: Mari Bolte
Designers: The Design Lab and Jaime Martens
Page Production: The Design Lab and Bobbie Nuytten
Photo Researcher: Eric Gohl
Cartographer: XNR Productions, Inc.
Library Consultant: Kathleen Baxter

Creative Director: Keith Griffin
Editorial Director: Nick Healy
Managing Editor: Catherine Neitge

Library of Congress Cataloging-in-Publication Data
Yackley-Franken, Nicki.
  Teens in Nepal / by Nicki Yackley-Franken.
     p. cm. — (Global connections)
  Includes index.
  ISBN 978-0-7565-3411-0 (library binding)
  1. Teenagers—Nepal—Social conditions—Juvenile literature. 2. Teenagers—Nepal—
Social life and customs—Juvenile literature. 3. Nepal—Social conditions—21st century—
Juvenile literature. 4. Nepal—Social life and customs—21st century—Juvenile literature. I.
Title. II. Series.
  HQ799.N36Y33 2008
  305.235095496—dc22   2007032693

Visit Compass Point Books on the Internet at www.compasspointbooks.com
or e-mail your request to custserv@compasspointbooks.com

Table of Contents

Kathmandu

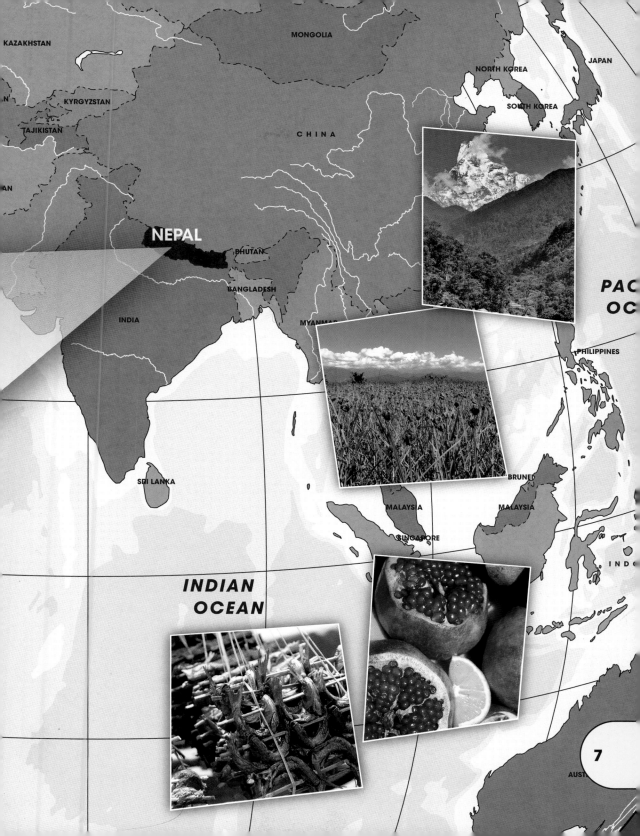

KAZAKHSTAN

MONGOLIA

KYRGYZSTAN

TAJIKISTAN

CHINA

NORTH KOREA

SOUTH KOREA

JAPAN

NEPAL

BHUTAN

BANGLADESH

INDIA

MYANMAR

PHILIPPINES

PAC
OC

SRI LANKA

BRUNEI

MALAYSIA

MALAYSIA

SINGAPORE

INDO

INDIAN
OCEAN

7

AUST

NEPAL IS A COUNTRY OF EXTREMES. Nepali teens live on towering snowcapped mountains and in lush tropical jungles. They also live in one of the poorest and least-developed nations in the world. Still, they can spend evenings watching MTV and talking on cell phones. They worship various gods, speak more than 100 languages, and belong to more than 60 ethnic groups. Some teens go to school, some are married, and some work full time in factories or rice fields.

Nepal has a long history of tolerance and acceptance. Teens embrace their country's diversity and treat one another with courtesy and respect. Today's teens make up the largest portion of Nepal's total population— 52 percent of the 28 million people living in the country are under the age of 18. This puts young people at the center of the southern Asian country's pursuit of change and advancement. The future of the country depends greatly on the actions and attitudes of the next generation.

The first Nepali school was founded in 1853. However, education has only been available to the general public since 1951.

CHAPTER ONE

The Future of Nepal

A GROUP OF 14-YEAR-OLD STUDENTS SITS ON HARD WOODEN BENCHES. They strain to hear their teacher's voice over the sound of wind rattling the building's tin roof. Separated by a narrow aisle, girls sit on one side of the room, and boys on the other. Students with notebooks try to take notes without elbowing the student next to them.

Though the room seems undersized for all 50 students, the closeness is a blessing because the building has no heat. The classroom walls, made of stone and mud, are bare except for a slate chalkboard in the front of the room on which the teacher writes the day's math lesson. Listening and rarely speaking, these students try to master the concept of long division. This is the way most students are taught—and while it may work for some, most find this form of learning difficult.

This is a typical classroom scene for Nepali teens, especially those who live in rural villages. Though a school with no electricity or running water may sound unpleasant, many students feel lucky to be there at all. According to the Nepali Ministry of Health, 11 percent of boys and 33 percent of girls ages 10 to 19 have never even been inside a school. Because of this, students do not let a few minor problems keep them from trying to get the most out of their time in class.

While it's true that most schools in Nepal are in bad shape, the situation is getting better. Fifty years ago, most

Why Can't They Go to School?

There are a number of obstacles keeping Nepali teens from attending school. The primary one is poverty. Some students cannot afford the fees for attending school, which are usually from 50 to 250 rupees (U.S. 80 cents to $3.85) a month. While it may not sound like much, this amount can be between 10 percent and more than 300 percent of a worker's monthly income. This is a high (and sometimes impossible) price for the poorest families. Private schools cost even more, from 1,300 rupees (U.S.$20) a month and up.

Many teens must work to help support their families. After food and clothing, education is the third-largest expense families face. Teens throughout Nepal wake every morning and go to work in the rice fields or in carpet factories instead of attending school. Girls are often expected to stay home to care for younger siblings and help around the house. Parents in Nepal are three times as likely to educate their sons as their daughters.

In 2006, Nepal's government spent nearly 6.5 billion rupees (U.S. $100 million) on education.

of these students wouldn't have had the chance to attend school. Public education in Nepal began in the early 1950s, and since that time the country has given more children the chance to learn. In 1951, only 300 schools and two colleges served a mere 10,000 students. Today there are more than 26,000 schools, 473 colleges, and five universities. These numbers continue to increase every year. In 2006, more than 1,770 schools were constructed in 50 districts of the country. These facilities do not reach every Nepali teen, but they do provide education for more than 6 million students.

The government has promised to improve education. By starting programs that increase the quality of the curriculum, teaching staff, and school facilities, it has taken the first step. The country now puts 15 percent of its annual budget into education, a record high. Eventually, it is hoped, this commitment will make education available to every Nepali youth.

Formal education in Nepal is split into three phases: primary, lower secondary, and upper secondary. The primary phase extends from first grade through fifth grade. Lower secondary covers grades six through eight. Upper secondary covers grades nine and 10. After grade 10, formal, mandatory education is complete. However, there has been a recent push for students to attend higher secondary schools. There they can complete grades 11 and 12 before entering college or finding a job.

Public School Problems

Most teens attend public schools, which are open to anyone. Primary education is the only phase that is truly free for all. Any community that wants its children to have additional education must build and keep up its own schools without help from the government.

Secondary students have to pay for textbooks, uniforms, and exam and maintenance fees. About 25 percent of the school's operating costs are paid by students in grades six and seven, and 50 percent of the costs are paid by students in grades eight through 11. This causes an uneven distribution of education facilities, and poor communities suffer the most. In addition, most schools can't provide a way for students to get to and from school, nor do they provide meals. These costs are the main reasons many teens don't attend secondary school.

Because not every village has a public school, some children must travel many miles on foot or by bicycle to attend school. In fact, some students must travel as many as six hours each day to get to and from the nearest school. Nepal's sometimes treacherous terrain can make travel difficult.

No public school buildings have air conditioning, and only some have running water. When the weather is

What to Wear

School dress codes vary from school to school. Most private and public schools require students to wear uniforms. However, students and their families must pay for the uniforms themselves. In most instances, male students wear matching shirts, pants, ties, and belts. Girls at the same school wear matching skirts, shirts, ties, and belts. A uniform can cost around 1,620 rupees (U.S.$25), a high price for the average family.

The climate of Nepal and poorly built schools can make learning difficult. In the summer, building temperatures can reach as high as 95 degrees Fahrenheit (35 degrees Celsius). In the winter, it can get as low as 40 F (2 C).

nice, teachers may hold classes outside, where there is more light and fresh air. In 2006, the Ministry of Education and Sports was forced to abandon a plan to construct low-quality, temporary school buildings after hearing complaints from people throughout the country. Proper buildings have been promised.

Public schools in bigger cities are usually better. These schools have more space, and some even contain a few computers. Still, classrooms in urban schools are often overcrowded and do not have reliable access to electricity.

In light of these problems, private education has become increasingly popular. Usually located in urban areas, private schools cater to middle-class families. But even rural families send their children to private schools if they

A Country Learns to Read

Public education is a new phenomenon in Nepal. The first school opened in 1853, but the school only served children of the ruling family. Public school was introduced in 1951, after the royal family was overthrown and a democratic system began. At that time, fewer than 5 percent of the population could read and only one of 100 children attended school. Today the literacy rate for ages 15 to 24 is nearly 76 percent and nearly 70 percent of young people go to school. Though the educational system still needs work, the country has made remarkable improvements in the last 50 years.

can afford it. These students often live at school during the school year, only returning home during festival breaks.

Generally, private schools offer the best instruction and facilities. Because they can afford to pay top salaries, they often employ better-educated teachers. Many can afford to build state-of-the-art campuses. It is not uncommon for teens attending a private school in

Kathmandu, Nepal's capital and largest city, to have access to a theater, gymnasiums, sports fields, and computer labs.

One reason many Nepalis prefer private education is that most private schools are "English medium" schools, meaning that teachers use the English language in the classroom. Throughout Nepal, people hold English education in higher regard than teaching done in the official Nepali language. Teens attending these private schools can usually speak fluent English by the time they graduate.

In the Classroom

The average school day for rural teens begins around 10 A.M., while urban teens usually begin around 8:30 A.M. Many rural students appreciate the later start time because they can help on the family farm before rushing off to school. Students attend approximately seven 45-minute class periods. Usually there is a short break between classes. But in some schools, students have just enough time between classes to walk from one room to the next. In other schools, teachers move from room to room, with students remaining in the same room. Students usually get an hourlong lunch break. Most schools do not serve lunch, so some teens bring their own, while others go home to eat. After lunch, students continue their studies. The school day ends between 3:30 P.M. and 5 P.M. Classes are held Sundays through Fridays, but many schools dismiss students after only half a day on Fridays.

According to the Ministry of Education and Sports, the student-to-teacher ratio throughout the country is 36 students for every teacher. In some schools, rooms are packed with as many as 75 students. These oversized classes sometimes create a difficult learning environment. Students do not get many chances to ask questions or get individual attention from teachers. As a result,

Although many school officials are interested in offering computer education and technology, very few schools can afford computers.

Government schools have very few books other than textbooks. The books they do have are usually left by travelers and are written in English or other foreign languages, rather than Nepali.

most students spend their seven class periods a day listening and taking notes, but not really participating.

More students also means more distractions. Teens often chat with each other during lectures or even leave before the class has ended. Sitting shoulder to shoulder with other students has also tempted many teens to cheat— a problem that has become rampant in Nepali schools.

What to Study

The curriculum in Nepali public schools was created with assistance from the United Nations Educational, Scientific, and Cultural Organization (UNESCO). The curriculum of U.S. schools has greatly influenced it as well. Both lower- and upper-secondary students usually study English, math, science, health, physical education, social studies, and geography. The study of Nepali language is compulsory. Elective courses like art, architecture, accounting, yoga, and various foreign languages are also offered. In recent years, the government has added vocational-training courses to the secondary-school curriculum to prepare students for skilled labor like office work or woodworking.

When the school day ends, homework begins. Many students spend one to five hours each day studying and working on assignments. The time spent depends on the student's commitment to success, available time, and other family or household responsibilities.

Generally students take exams during the school year. They take a comprehensive final test at the end of each year that determines whether they will be allowed to enter the next grade. There is a great deal of pressure to pass

The Importance of Health Education

Health and nutrition education are immensely important in Nepal—one in 10 children die before their first birthday. More than 45 percent of adolescent girls suffer from anemia, or low red blood cell count, because of poor diets. And fewer than one-third of Nepali doctors choose to practice in rural villages. To counter this, teens learn about proper eating habits and hygiene, and they gain life-saving information about sexually transmitted diseases such as AIDS.

The country's Ministry of Health wants to improve the health education of young people throughout Nepal. It has begun planning for special programs that will teach young people about population control, reproductive health, and nutrition. There also are many nonprofit organizations at work in Nepal trying to increase access to medical care, nutritious foods, and clean water supplies.

Teen Scenes

In Kathmandu, a 15-year-old boy jumps on his gas-powered scooter and heads to his private school. His backpack is loaded down with books and homework, all of which are in English. Though he grew up speaking Nepali, he attends a school where English is the only language used. School lasts for about eight hours and concentrates on subjects like math, health, and computer technology. He hopes this will help him get into medical school someday. He knows he must work hard and stay focused on his studies if he wants to fulfill his dream. Unemployment rates are high in Nepal, even for the educated.

Miles away, a 14-year-old girl walks two hours from her mountain village to the nearest school. She makes this trip every day, but she doesn't mind the walk. Few teens in her village go to school, so she feels lucky. Her crumbling school building has no electricity or running water. Again, she doesn't mind. She has bigger things to worry about. She is in the seventh grade—the grade her sister was in when her family made her quit school and get married. This teen knows she must study hard and prove herself as a student if she wants to stay in school.

In Dharan, a 16-year-old boy spends 15 hours a day working in a brick factory. He has never attended school and knows he never will. At the factory, he forms as many as 1,500 clay bricks a day. His job is difficult, requiring long hours and lots of physical labor.

He has arthritis, an ailment characterized by joint inflammation that leads to pain, swelling, stiffness in his hands, and constant back trouble from his job. But his family can't afford to send him to the doctor. Every day is filled with pain and hard work, but he tries to keep a good attitude. He knows his wages help his widowed mother feed and care for his four brothers and sisters.

The experiences of teens in Nepal vary tremendously. Some spend their days in school, others in factories. For most teens in Nepal, life isn't easy.

Enrollment for girls is less than 35 percent in secondary school.

these exams, so many teens spend hours poring over notes and textbooks beforehand.

At the end of 10th grade, students attempt to pass the most important exam of the year. In 2006, 46.5 percent of students were successful in passing, earning the School Leaving Certificate. After passing the exam, teens are considered adults and have the choice to continue their education or enter the work force.

Gaining this certificate often brings great pride to teenagers and their families. Proud parents will even host a party, inviting relatives and friends to help celebrate their teen's success. Those who pass this exam undoubtedly feel

fortunate to be among the few in their country who have had such a chance.

One Nepali teen said that receiving an education and earning his certificate have given him tremendous confidence for the future:

I feel I am better off than the people who haven't been to school. I feel I have had a good chance in my life by being able to go to school. … Now since I will be having my education certificates, I think it will be very easy for me to apply for jobs.

He knows he is lucky to have had the chance to go to school, and he feels ready and prepared to take on the world of work.

Nepal is one of the few countries in the world where men have a higher life expectancy than women.

2

The Diversity of Daily Life

WALKING HOME FROM SCHOOL, A NEPALI TEEN LIVING IN KATHMANDU MAY PASS TOWERING TEMPLES, colorful palaces, and open-air markets selling fresh vegetables. Later he may go by single-family homes with satellite dishes and a pizzeria with an English name. Another teen of the same age living hundreds of miles away sees a much different scene. She sees almost nothing for miles except towering mountains and plunging canyons. There are no roads for her to walk on. She strides along mountain edges and across narrow wooden bridges. These two teens represent two very different lifestyles: life in the city and life in the country.

Rural Life

Today more than 85 percent of the country's population lives in rural settings. Some live in small valleys, some on mountainsides, and some in tropical jungles. Nearly 77 percent of Nepal's terrain consists of the mountain region or hill region. The highest one-third of the country is at an altitude above 10,000 feet (3,050 meters). Rural families living in the mountain and hill regions often remain isolated from the rest of the country. The mountainous landscape and lack of road-

23

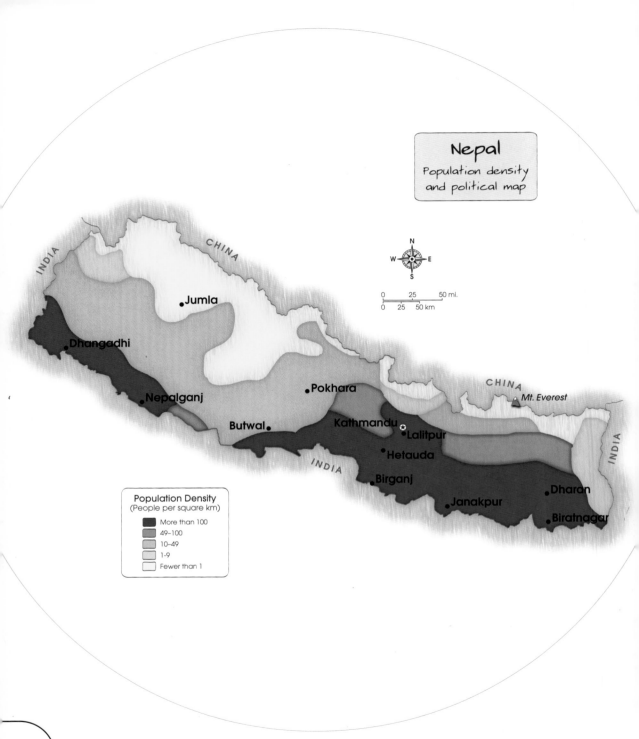

Nepal
Population density and political map

Jumla

Dhangadhi

Nepalganj

Pokhara

Butwal

Kathmandu

Lalitpur

Hetauda

Birganj

Janakpur

Dharan

Biratnagar

Mt. Everest

CHINA

CHINA

INDIA

INDIA

INDIA

N
W · E
S

0   25   50 mi.
0   25   50 km

Population Density
(People per square km)

■	More than 100
■	49–100
■	10–49
■	1-9
□	Fewer than 1

ways make travel difficult and access to many modern luxuries nearly impossible.

Many rural teens have never seen an airplane, never watched television, and never flushed a toilet. Overall, about 35 percent of the population lives in homes with no electricity. Even in homes that do have access to electricity, the service is not reliable. Blackouts are common, leaving whole cities, villages, and neighborhoods without power, sometimes for days. Also, a mere 37 percent of families have access to safe water supplies.

Some rural villagers may walk up to six hours for fresh water each day. Contaminated water is responsible for at least 80 percent of the country's illnesses.

Rural teens in the Tarai, Nepal's only flat-land region, also lack many luxuries of modern living. The Tarai is a lowland region with dense jungles and forests. Monsoons (winds that bring heavy rains) from June to September often cause the Himalayan rivers and streams to swell, leading to devastating floods. The annual rainfall in Nepal averages around 68 inches (173 centimeters); however, some areas of Nepal receive much more or less precipitation than others. For instance, in the southern part of the country, 210 inches (533 cm) is a more common average, while 10 inches (25.4 cm) is standard in the mountainous region of the north. The heaviest rainfall often causes floods that have been known to carry away homes and even wipe out whole villages. Repeated natural disasters keep the country from modernizing much of the area.

Rural teens have to work hard to ensure their basic survival. There are more than 3 million working children in the country. They grow, harvest, and

The Himalayas

Nepal's northern border consists of the Himalayas, the world's tallest mountain range. The range covers 229,500 square miles (596,700 square kilometers) in several countries. It crosses the entire length of Nepal, which is home to the tallest portion of the range. Eight of the 10 tallest mountains in the world are within the country's borders. The range's mountain passes (the low places between peaks) are high, too—usually above 15,000 feet (4,575 m). Some of the passes are so high, and so cold, that many glaciers can be found there.

Mount Everest	29,029 feet (8,854 m)
Kanchanjanga	28,209 feet (8,604 m)
Lhotse	27,940 feet (8,522 m)
Makalu	27,766 feet (8,469 m)
Cho Oyu	26,906 feet (8,206 m)

Many rural villagers must walk long distances to purchase food.

cook food. They make, wash, and repair clothes. Most teens wake up early to begin the chores that are vital to their livelihoods. Teens can be seen walking through the countryside to fetch water from wells, taps, or streams as early as 6 A.M. Other teens wake before the sun to work in the fields or herd livestock. Girls spend their mornings cooking breakfast, washing clothes, and taking care of siblings.

City Life

Life for urban teens is a bit easier. Their homes are more likely to have electricity and to be near a water supply. At markets and modern grocery stores, they can buy food instead of having to survive on what the family grows.

Urban teens usually have more time during the day for fun. They meet their friends to play sports or, if they can afford it, watch the newest Indian movie

Kathmandu Valley

Kathmandu Valley is an urban area in the central hill region of Nepal. It is made up of three cities: the capital of Kathmandu, Lalitpur (or Patan), and Bhaktapur. Nearly 1.5 million people live here. The valley, which sits at an altitude of about 4,000 feet (1,200 m), is often considered the cultural and political center of Nepal. Because it is surrounded by tall peaks, air pollution has become a serious problem. The bowl shape of the valley traps the chemicals from industries and vehicles in the valley. A haze of pollutants often fills the air. In the last 10 years, city hospitals have seen an increase in the number of respiratory infections, most likely because of increased air pollution. The most common ailment for adults is chronic bronchitis, a lung disease. The most common for children is asthma, another lung disease. Recently people in the valley have started wearing masks to protect themselves from the harmful smog and dust in the atmosphere.

Urban teens are more prone to smoke than those in rural areas. By the age of 20, about 35 percent of Nepali boys are smokers. The number of girls who smoke is much lower.

at the theater. Restaurants and coffee shops also are popular meeting places for city teens.

Like their rural counterparts, most urban teens are poor, and they have to work hard. The average income for a Nepali worker is 12,940 rupees (U.S.$200) a year. Even though families may have access to electricity and

more hours a day. Their jobs include making clothing and carpeting that will be sold to European buyers and tourists, and making bricks that are often purchased by the government or by private contracting companies.

Home Sweet Home

Wealthy urban teens may live in Western-style homes with porches and lovely landscaping. However, there are few wealthy and middle-class families. The majority of city teens live in small houses or apartments without refrigerators, stoves, or washing machines. When they wake in the morning, their toes likely do not sink into soft, warm carpet but instead hit hard concrete floors. To use the bathroom, they walk out the front door and through a courtyard to a restroom, which is often nothing more than an outhouse that is shared by the whole neighborhood.

Nepal's climate extremes have a big impact on where and how rural teens live. Subzero temperatures and heavy snowfall are common in the Himalayas. Here families usually live close to their neighbors. In fact, most mountain homes are stacked on top of each other, and many share a wall with the home next to them. This closeness helps to keep the cold out and the heat in. In contrast, teens living in the Tarai experience a subtropical climate. Here summer temperatures peak around 113 F (45 C). Homes are built on stilts to protect the inhabitants from wild animals and floods.

indoor plumbing, they may not be able to afford the services. Many urban teens still have to spend at least part of their day working in gardens or on farms, cooking, cleaning, or fetching firewood.

Some urban teens work outside the home as domestic help, store clerks, or factory workers. These teens do not attend school, but instead work 12 or

The Nepali people are dependent on plant resources. More than 85 percent of the rural population uses natural herbal remedies as their form of health care.

Rural families may share their living spaces with livestock. Animals live under the houses of families in the Tarai. In mountain homes, sheep and goats often live on the first floor of the home. The family lives on the second floor. This benefits both the animals and the family. Being indoors keeps the animals from freezing, and in turn, the animals help keep the family warm.

Religion and Everyday Life

Until April 2007, Nepal was the only country in the world that officially called itself a Hindu state. Since then, it has been declared a secular, or nonreligious, state. This decision received a mixed reaction. Hindus wonder whether cows, which are considered holy and are the national animal of Nepal, will remain sacred. About 80 percent of the population follows Hinduism. For this reason, Hinduism plays a strong role in Nepali daily life. Most teens see Hindu shrines and statues of gods and goddesses at every turn. Each morning, countless people rush through streets and along country trails to the nearest shrine for *puja*, or worship. The remaining 20 percent of the population has welcomed the decision as a positive step for ethnic minorities and a step away from the social division created by Nepal's caste system.

The caste system separates members of society based on their family's tribe or

puja
poo-jya

Kathmandu's Durbar Square is home to the Royal Kumari, or Living Goddess, of Nepal. It also contains shrines honoring the Hindu gods Parvati and Shiva.

A Home For All

Nepal is home to more than 60 ethnic groups that speak 100 languages. Most groups have remained in one region of Nepal for centuries. For instance, most Sherpas have lived in the mountain region for about 500 years. The Newars have lived in the Kathmandu Valley for 1,500 years. Many ethnic groups speak their own languages, follow their own customs, and celebrate a number of their own holidays and festivals.

Ethnic Groups of Nepal

Himalaya region:
Sherpa, Manangba, Lopi, Thakali, Tamang

Hill region:
Magar, Gurung, Newar, Rai, Thami, Limbu

Tarai region:
Tharu, Awadhi, Dhimal, Danuwar, Bhojpuri, Maithili

history in the country. Often members of different castes aren't allowed to associate with each other. Practiced in Nepal since the 1300s, the caste system comes from the country's Hindu roots. Nepal's caste system is unique in that indigenous and tribal people are classified. These people make up nearly 40 percent of the population and do not follow the Hindu religion. Main castes include Brahmin (the priestly class), Chhetri (rulers and warriors), Vaishya (merchants, artisans, and landowners), and Shudra (farmers and laborers). There are also the Untouchables—sometimes referred to as Dalits. Untouchables are denied use of certain temples, restaurants, shops, water sources, and other public areas.

In 1962, the government ruled that discrimination against low castes was illegal. In the past, people treated Untouchables with disdain and intolerance. Marriages between castes almost never took place. Although the system has become less important in recent years, discrimination against Untouchables has remained strong. The majority of Nepalis whose income falls below the poverty line belong to the Untouchable caste. In some areas and within certain ethnic groups, the caste system remains a major social force.

The Buddhist religion also influences the way Nepali people live. Less than 11 percent of the population follows Buddhism, but its presence can be seen everywhere. Colorful prayer flags, signifying the location of a Buddhist

Buddhism is the dominant religion in northern Nepal.

place of worship, adorn urban and rural landscapes. Buddhism has its roots in Nepal because the Buddha, Siddhartha Gautama, was born in 563 B.C. in Lumbini, a Tarai village. To this day, Nepali teens of all religions participate in a festival celebrating Buddha's birth. Unlike many people in the world, Nepali citizens respect other religions. Hindus, Buddhists, Muslims, and Christians have peacefully coexisted in Nepal for hundreds of years.

33

Hinduism

Hinduism is one of the oldest religions in the world, and the number-one religion in Nepal.

Hinduism is a polytheistic religion—its followers worship multiple gods and goddesses. Generally Hindus recognize three main gods: Brahma (the creator), Vishnu (the preserver), and Shiva (the destroyer). Other deities they worship are considered forms of one of these three. Nepali cities and villages are filled with shrines, temples, and statues for these three Hindu gods.

The major beliefs of Hindus revolve around the idea that a Hindu's actions on Earth, including his or her devotion to the gods, will determine the person's position in the next life. Hindus believe in reincarnation. A person who is evil in one life might be reborn as an insect or low-caste member. Good deeds, on the other hand, should lead to happiness and high-class living in the next life. Because Hindus earn their status, they are taught to accept their place in this life and hope to earn better in the next. The death and rebirth cycle is not endless. A person can be released into *moksha* if the highest level of devotion and personal clarity are attained. Moksha is similar to the Christian idea of heaven and the Buddhist idea of nirvana.

moksha
mok-sha

Hinduism is quite tolerant of other religions, even allowing Hindus to practice other religions. In Nepal, many people follow a combination of Hinduism and Buddhism.

Food and Drink

Religion also affects the food served at meals. For instance, cows are sacred in the Hindu religion, so most teens do not eat beef. In fact, cows are protected by law. The penalty for killing a cow is the same as for killing a person. The crime is punishable by up to 12 years in jail. Throughout Nepal, cows wander around city streets and rest in front of ancient temples and modern shopping marts. Restaurants that do serve beef cater mainly to foreign tourists and have to import the meat from other countries.

Meat in general is a delicacy for most teens in the country. Goat, chicken, and mutton are the most common. Many teens only eat these delicacies on festival occasions. On ordinary days, rice and lentils are common. Lentils are the flat seeds of the lentil plant, which is grown throughout the country. Water buffalo meat, *momos*, or stuffed dumplings, and *alu dam,* or spicy fried potatoes, are also well-liked dishes.

Momos are most often filled with buffalo, chicken, vegetables, or a soft cheese.

Eating in restaurants is popular among teens who can afford it. Pizza—made with toppings such as yak or goat cheese, garlic, eggplant, and eggs—has become a favorite food of many. Western fast-food chains have not yet made their way into Nepal.

The most popular drink in Nepal is tea. It is a staple in the Nepali diet and has been for centuries. Most teens drink tea at every meal and with snacks. In the last 20 years, life for teens in Nepal has evolved a great deal, but the tradition of tea has not changed. Water must be boiled to make it safe to drink, and many diners drink their water hot and plain or with tea leaves. Bottled drinks are especially popular with teens.

alu dam
aloo dumb

Nepali life is highly focused on the family.

3

The Importance of Family

FOR HUNDREDS OF YEARS, NEPALI TEENS HAVE LIVED WITH THEIR PARENTS AND SIBLINGS, AS WELL AS THEIR GRANDPARENTS, AUNTS, UNCLES, AND COUSINS. The family impacts how and with whom most teens spend their time, and much of daily life centers on the family. Friends are important to teens in Nepal as well, but most socializing still takes place among relatives.

The average rural teen in Nepal has four or five brothers and sisters, while urban teens have only one or two. With their siblings, cousins, and other extended family nearby, rural and urban teens seldom lack company. However, they do lack privacy, something that simply does not exist for some. On an average day, homes fill with the sounds of children playing, relatives talking, women cooking, and men discussing business.

Because families are close, teens often have special relationships with extended family members. They refer to cousins as "brothers and sisters" and aunts and uncles as "mothers and fathers." Grandparents also play an important role. Old age is seen as a time of relaxation and meditation. Young Nepalis are expected to treat their

Children are an important part of the family. They entertain, help around the house, and are expected to care for their parents in their old age.

grandparents with proper respect and admiration, and they listen with rapt attention to stories of family history.

Living in joint families teaches generosity, tolerance, and respect. The livelihood of the entire family depends on all members' working hard, fulfilling their responsibilities, and putting the group first. Family loyalty and the importance of working together are stressed. All members of the family own the land and combine their money to support the entire household. Consequently there is no sense of "yours" or "mine." Selfishness is one of the worst traits a teen could demonstrate.

Changes in the Family

Family dynamics in Nepal have begun changing in the last 10 years. Families now might live in single-family homes instead of extended-family households. This is especially true in urban areas. Economic strains forced many parents to move to another town or city where jobs are easier to find. Western influences through the media and English education also have contributed to this change.

Many people try to imitate the Western nuclear family of two parents and their children. This new, smaller family model will probably lead to a change in the country's population growth and makeup. Currently the population of Nepal grows at a rate of about 2 percent a year. The population is overwhelmingly young, with 52 percent under the age of 18. If the Nepalis keep following the Western family model, growth will slow down, and the population will likely become older.

Those parents who do move away from the extended family usually try to keep teens connected to their roots. Nepali teenagers and their families typically travel twice a week to visit relatives if they live in the same general area. Even extended families living hundreds of miles apart come together to celebrate festivals and holidays. These festivals take place at least once a month. Many of them give families an opportunity to eat together, play together, and catch up on family news.

Universal Happiness

From a young age, Nepali teens are taught to remain content despite difficult living situations. The happiness of each member of a family is important for the happiness of all members. For this reason, the Nepalis are known across the globe for their friendliness.

The culture's greeting of "*Namaste*" adds to the land's friendliness. When two people meet on the street, both bring their palms together below their chin, bow their head slightly, smile, and say "Namaste," which literally means, "I bow to the god in you." This greeting reinforces the Hindu ideal that there is divinity, or godly power, in everything and everyone.

Namaste
na-ma-stay

Most decisions involving the family are made by men.

Gender Roles in the Family

Nepal has always had a patriarchal, or male-dominated, society. This emphasis holds strong today. In traditional families, the oldest male—whether he is the father, grandfather, or uncle—holds the title as head of household. He has the final say in many important decisions affecting his family, including whether teens go to school and whom teens will marry. The head of household also decides how a family's money is spent.

No Equality for Women

More than 20 laws in Nepal discriminate against women. Some religious groups do not consider women human and respond to the birth of a girl by saying, "Nothing was born." At least 75 percent of women have been subjected to some form of abuse at home. Both boys and girls feel that a man has the right to beat his wife under certain circumstances, such as not looking after her children properly or being disrespectful to her husband's family.

The Language of Conversation

Many Nepali teens speak two or three languages. Growing up, many teens speak the language of their native ethnic group. At school, most teens are taught in Nepali, the official language of Nepal. Nearly everyone who attends school also learns English, which is spoken in many government and business offices. Many also understand and speak Hindi from watching Indian TV.

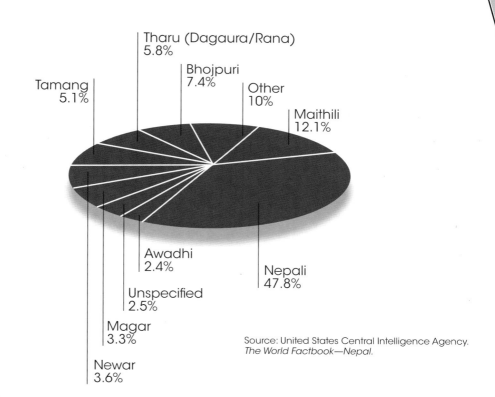

Tharu (Dagaura/Rana)
5.8%

Bhojpuri
7.4%

Other
10%

Maithili
12.1%

Tamang
5.1%

Awadhi
2.4%

Nepali
47.8%

Unspecified
2.5%

Magar
3.3%

Newar
3.6%

Source: United States Central Intelligence Agency. *The World Factbook—Nepal.*

The average Nepali woman has four children. Many Hindu women wear forehead adornments called tika—some of them very large.

Women and children are expected to remain obedient to men. Women of all ages have a secondary position of power behind their fathers, husbands, brothers, and even their sons.

The family chain of command, with men at the top, also affects the relationship between brothers and sisters. In general, girls receive less education and fewer opportunities than their brothers. Parents tend to be much more permissive and generous with sons. Girls are given less medical care and, in poorer families, less food.

In general, the family raises girls to become housekeepers and mothers, while boys grow up to be wage earners and authority figures. Even though many middle-income families send their daughters to good schools, the family will still expect them to take on their traditional female roles when they finish.

Social Lives

Because most Nepalis live in small rural villages with few facilities for entertainment, socializing takes place among family members and close friends. In the hill and Himalayan regions, a home's fireplace is the social center. Family members gather around the fire, especially during cold winter evenings, to drink tea, share stories, sing songs, and laugh together. For families with access to electricity, the fire has been

Getting Around

Getting from place to place is not always easy for Nepali teens. High mountains, rushing rivers, and dense jungles make it almost impossible to create roads in much of the countryside. The country's first paved road wasn't built until 1956. Since that time, the country has constructed 9,900 miles (3,020 m) of roads, a little more than half of them paved. There are, however, still villages where teens have to travel many miles along unpaved trails before arriving at one of Nepal's few major highways.

For most teens, the primary form of transportation remains their two feet. Teens walk to school, work, and their friends' homes, and back again. Some teens may have bicycles or may be able to rent a rickshaw, a cart that seats one or two people and is powered by either an engine or a human runner.

In cities, most teens use public transportation, such as buses or occasionally taxis. Some urban teens, especially boys, speed through town on their gas-powered scooters. The wealthiest teens drive cars. Those lucky enough to have access to a vehicle are eligible to take the driver's exam and receive a license at 16.

replaced by the television. Families sit around the TV and watch Nepali channels or, if the family has a satellite dish, American or Indian movies.

Visiting family members is a common pastime for urban teens and their families. They take the bus, walk, or, if they're wealthy, drive a car to a relative's home. Together with their extended families, teens might play soccer or basketball outside or stay inside visiting and watching television.

Urban teens do not spend as much time working as their rural counterparts, which leaves them more time for friends. One Kathmandu girl said that friends are central to her social life:

When someone reaches the teenage years, friends become more important than family because we think the same as our friends and our choices match with those of our friends. It becomes easier to get along with friends than family.

Popular names

You've got a popular name in Nepal if you're called Krishna or Sita. The following are some of the most common Nepali names. Some names have meanings, while others are names of gods and goddesses.

Boys

Name	Meaning
Krishna	Name of Hindu god
Ram	Name of king of India
Hari	Name of Hindu god
Kedar	Ash
Pema	Lotus flower
Shyam	Name of Hindu god

Girls

Name	Meaning
Sita	Name of wife of Ram
Laxmi	Name of Hindu goddess
Anita	Grace; variety
Shanti	Peace
Tara	Name of Hindu goddess
Rita	Order or course of things

More than 20 percent of girls are married before they reach the age of 16.

Today most urban teens have groups of friends about their age to spend time with on weekends or after school.

Friendships between boys and girls have become common during the last five to 10 years. Traditionally girls were expected to socialize only with other girls, and boys were only to socialize with other boys. Nepali society was concerned that allowing boys and girls to spend unchaperoned time together could lead to premarital sex, ruining a daughter's honor and the honor of her family. While there is still some fear of dishonor attached to these friendships, today that suspicion has lessened.

Although public displays of affection are viewed as culturally unacceptable, they still occur.

Social dating between young people is taboo and usually happens in secret. Public displays of affection are considered inappropriate. Teens are rarely seen holding hands, hugging, or kissing in public. In the hill region, however, teens flirt more openly because the society tends to be less conservative.

Almost all teens are at home in bed by 10 P.M. In cities and villages, most businesses close before this time. Streets and neighborhoods are empty. Throughout Nepal, night visiting is discouraged. In recent years, night has been considered an especially dangerous time for teens to be out because of a political rebellion that has resulted in violence, kidnappings, and even deaths.

The People's War

In 1996, the Communist Party of Nepal, called the Maoist faction, organized a movement against Nepal's constitutional monarchy. Between 1996 and 2006, the movement spread its message of violence throughout the country. Members hoped to abolish the monarchy, controlled by King Gyanendra, and establish a communist state.

The rebellion affected virtually every part of teen life in Nepal. At its height, the Maoist army controlled 75 percent of the country's territory—everything except cities, towns, and government buildings. Almost 13,000 citizens died as a result of Maoist violence. Thousands more fled the countryside for Nepal's cities or foreign countries. In rural communities, teens had to be especially careful. Rural areas experienced more attacks than urban regions. Also, 25 percent to 30 percent of children under 18 were recruited or stolen from their homes to serve in the Maoist army. For this reason, teens throughout the country generally tried to stay indoors after nightfall.

A movement toward peace began in April 2006 when a massive People's Movement and the reinstated government stripped King Gyanendra of all ruling power. The king was reduced from the country's direct ruler to a figurehead only. After about eight months of peace talks and cease-fires, the People's War officially came to an end on November 21, 2006. Girija Prasad Koirala, Nepal's prime minister at the time, signed a comprehensive peace accord with the Maoist leadership. The agreement allowed the Maoists to participate in the country's new democratic government. In January 2007, the country officially changed from a constitutional monarchy to a parliamentary democracy.

Hindu women pray for marital bliss, the well-being of their spouses and children, and the purification of their bodies and souls. Single women wish for a good husband.

4

Having a Festive Time

A NEPALI TEEN, WEARING HER NEW RED SARI, STANDS IN LINE BEHIND HER YOUNGER BROTHERS, SISTERS, AND COUSINS. She watches as her grandfather dabs his finger in a mixture of rice, yogurt, and red food coloring. She smiles as he marks the forehead of her youngest brother. This mark is called tika and is given by the oldest member of the household to the younger members. The girl has spent the entire week celebrating Dashain with family and friends. On this final day of the holiday, the teen—like teens throughout Nepal—has traveled to the home of her oldest relative so she can receive this important blessing. As her turn arrives, she feels a sense of pride and family loyalty as she bows her head, allowing her grandfather to give her tika.

For many teens, there are more festivals and holidays than ordinary days on the calendar. Government holidays, Buddhist and Hindu holidays, and local village holidays are all celebrated. Some festivals

tika
tee-ka

Buddhist devotees light more than 150,000 candles during one of Nepal's many holidays.

are national, some are local or regional, and some are religious.

An average of three festivals a month are celebrated. They range from multiple-day events jam-packed with entertainment, food, and worshipping to smaller, more reserved get-togethers that include only the family and a day of visiting. At many of these festivals, friends and family join to perform traditional dances. These are the same dances their ancestors performed hundreds of years ago.

Dashain

Lasting 10 days, Dashain is the longest and most important Hindu holiday in Nepal. It usually falls in September or October. However, the festival dates vary from year to year because the

Calendar of Holidays

There are 12 months in the Nepali calendar. Each month begins around the middle of the month on the Gregorian calendar, which is used in most of the world. Festival dates vary from year to year because they are determined by a lunar calendar. The major Nepali holidays and festivals are:

FESTIVALS	MONTHS
Valentine's Day	February
Holi	February or March
Naya Barsa (New Year)	March or April
Buddha's Birthday	May or June
Janai Purnima	July or August
Raksha Bandhan	July or August
Tij	August or September
Indra Jatra	August or September
Dashain	September or October
Tihar	October or November

timing of Hindu festivals is determined by the lunar calendar, which is based on the cycle of the moon. During Dashain, schools are closed for 15 days, and government offices are closed for seven to eight days. Teens spend time with family and friends, enjoying parades, carnivals, religious rituals, and lots of good food.

On this holiday, families try to be together. Days before the festival, trails in the mountains and hills become congested with travelers. Roadways fill with cars and buses taking city folk back to the country.

King Gyanendra gives Hindu followers *tika* during Dashain.

Families making these trips usually carry gifts for grandparents, brothers, sisters, cousins, and anyone else who may be present at the celebration. Most teens both give and receive gifts during the festival. Clothes are the most popular gifts, but money and sweets are also common. Despite the poverty many experience, gift giving is a major part of the festival. In fact, there is so much pressure to give lavish presents that many families go into debt doing it.

The first nine days of Dashain commemorate the victory of the Hindu goddess Durga over a demon who terrorized the Earth in the form of an enormous buffalo. To show their devotion to Durga, on the ninth day of Dashain each household sacrifices an animal, usually a goat, sheep, or buffalo. Boys typically help kill the animal, while girls help prepare and cook the meat. After offering a portion to the gods, the family enjoys a feast. Many look forward to this meal all year long because this may be one of the only times they eat meat.

On this day, teens in Kathmandu can witness a gruesomely spectacular event that commemorates Durga's triumph over the evil buffalo. Each year, people travel to Hanuman Dhoka, a famous public courtyard in the city, to watch the public sacrifice of hundreds of buffaloes. Thousands of people of all ages stand on the sidelines and cheer as the ritual takes place. By the end, onlookers stand ankle deep in blood. This ritual may seem harsh, but for the Nepalis it is a vital part of worshipping and celebrating Dashain.

Nepal's most important festival ends with the giving of tika on the 10th day. This day is filled with more feasting and more togetherness. It marks the end of an important spiritual and family-centered celebration.

Other Festivals

Teens do not have to wait long for the next big festival. Tihar is celebrated just one month after Dashain. This important Hindu festival lasts five days and takes place in October or November.

Like Dashain, Tihar is a festival of family bonding. Teens usually don't have school, and most parents don't work. The family spends time feasting, talking, and taking a break from the hard work of day-to-day life. For Hindus, this is a festival of religious devotion. They believe that everything and everyone is divine, so on Tihar they honor the holiness of certain animals, such as dogs and cows. Teens and other

Dogs are among the animals honored during Tihar.

Nepalis can be seen placing colorful flower necklaces around the animals' necks and putting tika on their foreheads.

On the third day, people worship Laxmi, the Hindu goddess of wealth. In Laxmi's honor, children help their families decorate the inside and outside of the house with oil lamps and candles. Villages can be seen miles away because of the shining homes.

The last day of the festival is probably the most important for teens. Brothers often travel as far as needed to receive a blessing from their sisters. The sister places tika on her brother and offers prayers for her brother's long, happy life. Then the two sit down together for a meal—probably of dumplings and potatoes or rice and lentils. This part of the festival keeps bonds between brothers and sisters strong.

In February or March, teens enjoy

Raksha Bandhan

Raksha Bandhan is another holiday that celebrates the relationship between brothers and sisters. A sister ties decorated silk around her brother's right wrist and gives him tika. Brothers give sisters gifts, like jewelry or new clothes, and promise to make sure the sister is always taken care of. If his sister is married, a brother may need to travel many miles to share this day with her.

During Raksha Bandhan, a member of the Brahmin caste oversees the celebration and is available to tie the silk thread around the wrist of everyone who wants it.

HAVING A FESTIVE TIME

Tij is an important festival for Nepali girls and women. On this day, they wear red, visit temples, and sing and dance with friends and relatives.

the festival of Holi, which lasts about one week. For many teens, this is the most lighthearted Hindu celebration. Often called the "festival of colors," this holiday allows teens to splatter colorful paints and powders on each other. The streets fill with people dancing and singing as they cover each other head-to-toe with bright colors. Merriment and laughter are the primary goals of Holi.

For Women Only

In August or September, women and girls have a festival just for them. Many girls look forward to this festival, called Tij, because it means three days away from the housework and fieldwork that consume most of their lives. On the first day, all women in the house come together for a feast. On the second day, they fast, and do not eat anything. The women hope their devotion will lead the gods to bless them with good marriages and many children. During the day, girls bathe in nearby rivers, dress in their best saris, and worship the Hindu god Shiva. After these rituals, they gather with friends and family to dance and sing into the night. This holiday is an excellent time for women to come together and build friendships.

Dashain, Tihar, Holi, and Tij are

Buddha's Birthday

Just over 10 percent of Nepal's population is Buddhist, but Buddhist holidays are celebrated with enthusiasm by people throughout Nepal. The most celebrated of these holidays is Buddha Jayanti, or Buddha's Birthday. For Nepali teens, Buddha Jayanti, in May or June, is a time for feasting and visiting friends and relatives. Large groups of people parade through the streets. Red, blue, yellow, and white flags—which represent the elements of fire, air, earth, and water—fly high above Buddhist homes.

Swayambhu Temple in Kathmandu is the center of the celebration. Millions of devout Buddhists from across the globe come to this ancient temple to renew their faith. This spot is one of the holiest Buddhist destinations in the world, but it is not easy to get to. Pilgrims must climb 300 steps to reach the shrine.

just a few of the Hindu festivals Nepali teens celebrate each year. Many non-Hindu holidays and festivals are celebrated as well, including Buddhist festivals and, most recently, the Western holiday of Valentine's Day. Festivals offer a break from the struggles of daily life and give teens something to look forward to in a land with few distractions. Participating in the festivals helps teens preserve their country's culture. According to one Nepali teen, "Nepalese teenagers are very enthusiastic, and they really love and respect their culture and country a lot." Taking part in the traditional rituals is one way they can show that respect.

Honoring Life's Big Moments

Throughout Nepal, teens also take part in more personal celebrations—ones that mark the major steps in their lives. The transition into adulthood is honored with special care and respect.

Almost every group in Nepal performs a coming-of-age ritual. These celebrations differ greatly from group to group. When a male of the Brahmin or Chhetri caste reaches puberty, for instance, he receives a sacred thread. He must wear the thread over his right shoulder and under his left arm. Receiving this signifies his movement into adulthood. Now he can eat with the other adult men in his family.

The coming of age of many Hindu girls is also an important event. A number of ethnic groups believe that a girl

The Ihi ceremony is performed between the ages of 5 and 11. It is done to prevent widowhood—because the girls are married to Vishnu, they will never become a widow.

must be isolated, usually locked away in a room, for a period of time when she reaches puberty. This is especially true among the Newars, an ethnic group that lives primarily in the Kathmandu Valley. A Newar girl undergoes Ihi, a mock-marriage to the Hindu god Vishnu. Following the ritual, the girl is usually locked in a room for 12 days when she menstruates for the first time. Newars, like many ethnic groups in Nepal, con-sider a menstruating woman unclean or polluted. When the girl emerges from her isolation, she is considered a woman. She takes on more responsibili-ties in the home, and the family may even begin to seek a husband for her.

Of Marrying Age

Teens in Nepal marry young. The average age for marriage is 19. Though the law forbids marriage before 18

57

Along with marrying young, Nepali women become mothers early as well. More than 40 percent of Nepali women are mothers by the time they turn 19.

without parental consent, the law is rarely enforced and child marriages do occur. Seven percent of girls in Nepal marry before the age of 10, 60 percent are married before the age of 20, and by age 25 more than 80 percent have found husbands.

Generally there are two types of marriages in Nepal: arranged marriages and love marriages. In arranged marriages, parents choose their children's partners. When a daughter or son nears marriage age, parents or other relatives start looking for a suitable spouse. Some parents even commit their children to marriage as infants. Brides and grooms in arranged engagements might be given the chance to accept or decline the pairing.

When couples meet, fall in love, become engaged, and marry, they enter a love marriage. These unions are becoming more common. Eloping is a new trend in Nepal. Teens tend to elope because they worry their parents will disapprove of their fiancé. The concept of love has become highly romanticized, and the secrecy of eloping is an appealing idea to many teens.

Like coming-of-age ceremonies, marriage ceremonies vary among groups. In general, weddings are multi-day events attended by family members and friends. In small villages, a wedding often becomes a villagewide affair, with everyone joining the celebration. Traditional Nepali weddings begin with the bride, groom, and guests gathering at the groom's home, where a ceremony takes place. The entire group then walks together to the home of the bride, where a number of rituals are performed, including the groom's giving tika to the bride. The red tika often matches the bride's bright red sari. Gambling, feasting, and dancing take place at the bride's home. The bride and groom then lead a procession back to the groom's home. Once she marries, a bride joins her husband's family, usually living under the same roof as her in-laws.

Soon after marriage, the couple is expected to start a family. In fact, if a woman does not have a baby, she risks bringing shame upon her family. Many adults claim that they believe a married couple should wait two to four years to have a child, to enable them to save enough money to support and raise the child. However, adults also value fertility and don't believe in using birth control so soon after marriage. Although 98 percent of the population is aware of at least one birth control method, only 35 percent have actually used any form of contraception. As a result, many women become pregnant right away, and most teen brides become teen mothers. And, though many women see two or three children as the ideal family size, four or five children are the reality because of the lack of family planning. Starting a family is the final step in the transformation from adolescence to adulthood.

Multiple Wives

One Nepali girl said:

If girls don't have a baby within the first year of marriage, they must answer to accusations of infertility raised by society. Sometimes they fear that if they do not have a baby on time, the husband might marry other women.

Polygamy, or the practice of having more than one spouse, has been illegal in Nepal since 1963. However, men can take a second wife if the first wife is suffering from an incurable disease; is insane, paralyzed, or blind; has failed to give birth within the first 10 years of marriage; or agrees to live separately after receiving a share of her husband's property. Most women are unaware that polygamy is illegal in Nepal. The polygamists can serve one to three years in jail and be fined 25,000 rupees (U.S.$385). Those women who are aware that it's illegal don't want to see their husbands punished since the husbands will still be responsible for providing for their wives.

Nepali girls ages 10 to 14 work twice as much as boys in the same age group.

5

Working Hard

NEPAL IS THE 12TH-POOR-EST COUNTRY IN THE WORLD, WITH NEARLY 40 PERCENT OF ITS POPULA-TION LIVING ON LESS THAN 65 RUPEES (U.S.$1) A DAY. This reality makes it necessary for almost every teen to work both inside and outside the home. In fact, most children begin working as young as 6. Parents have no choice—they must send their children to work because the family needs money in order to survive. In a land where few people have the luxury of eating three meals a day and many go to bed hungry, every single family member must contribute. For urban and rural teens, hard work is a fundamental part of growing up in Nepal.

Today it is estimated that 2.6 million Nepalis ages 5 to 14 participate in Nepal's labor force. Nearly 2 million of these young people work full time. While these numbers may seem high, they are con-siderably lower than 10 years ago. Fewer teenagers work full time today than ever before. This may be because more and more parents send their teens to school, which limits the time they can work.

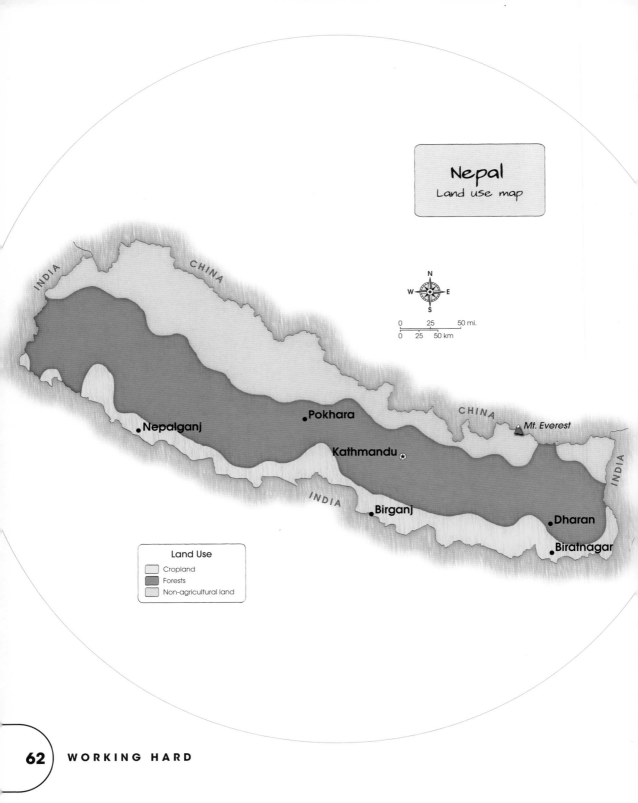

Nepal
Land use map

N
W E
S

0   25   50 mi.
0   25 50 km

INDIA

CHINA

CHINA

Mt. Everest

INDIA

Pokhara

Nepalganj

Kathmandu

INDIA

Birganj

Dharan

Biratnagar

Land Use
Cropland
Forests
Non-agricultural land

On the Farm

Currently more than 75 percent of Nepal's population earns an income from agriculture. Teens may work all day and into the evening planting, plowing, or harvesting fields of rice, corn, millet, or sugarcane. Rice is the most common crop, accounting for 55 percent of all crops grown in Nepal.

Most teens working in the fields do not have access to modern farm machinery. Instead of steering a planter attached to an engine-powered tractor, as farmers do in the West, a Nepali teen walks to the field in the morning with a group of oxen. The oxen, fastened shoulder to shoulder, slowly pull small, often old, equipment across the field.

Girls also work on the farm. Women do most of the weeding,

Farming with oxen is the only method used in Nepal. Even this is getting expensive, with oxen costing from 200 rupees to 2,000 rupees (U.S. $3.10 to $30.90).

harvesting, and distributing of crops. Of course, this is all done by hand. Teen girls may spend hours, sometimes whole days, under the hot sun picking the ripe rice stalks or the golden wheat. This continual bending and standing is physically demanding work. And the work often does not end there; workers also may have to distribute the produce. For instance, after harvesting rice, girls must often carry the 10-foot-tall (3 m) bundles of stalks on their backs to their homes or the homes of their employer.

In the mountain region, the landscape makes it difficult for crops to grow, so many families work as herders.

A Woman's Work Is Never Done

Women in Nepal usually work harder and longer than men. So most women, teens included, wake up early to start housework. Without modern appliances, most women must wash clothes and dishes by hand. They do the cooking over a fire or a small burner. Also, because men do little to help raise the children, women have that responsibility, too.

For many women, taking care of children and housework is just one part of their workday. Female teens going to school are expected to help around the house as much as possible when not in class. In rural areas, teenage daughters and their mothers often work in the fields or create handicrafts, such as baskets or jewelry, that can be sold for profit. In fact, women do about 70 percent of the work in a village. In the city, women are employed as factory workers, domestic servants, teachers, or store clerks. Then, after spending the day working, a woman returns home to continue her seemingly endless household tasks. The hard work of women may be a key reason Nepal is one of the few countries in the world where men live longer than women.

Families living at Nepal's highest altitudes may spend their days taking herds of sheep, goats, cattle, or yaks to graze. Livestock provides milk and food for the farmer, and animal dung serves as a source of fuel.

Though they work hard, most farmers earn little, if any, spending cash. Most farmers only raise enough food to feed their family. These families farm for survival. Some do try to make a living through farming, but the sons and daughters usually do not receive an actual wage. The money from the harvest goes to provide for the entire family's basic needs.

In the Factory

Most factory employees older than 16 work long hours—they can average 15-hour workdays for the entire week. Most factory workers are found in carpet, clothing, or brick plants. The work is often repetitive and physically straining. A teen working in a brick factory, for instance, may spend the entire day filling brick molds, scraping off excess mud, and tapping the molds against the hard ground so the bricks will hold their form. The repetitiveness of the work, the constant dampness, and the long hours outside often lead to fever, coughing, and joint problems.

Nepali teens work in stone quarries, make bricks, carry heavy loads as porters, and weave carpets.

65

Child Labor

On January 11, 2003, Nepali police rescued 14 boys and girls ages 14 to 17 who were forced to work as spinners at a factory in Kathmandu. They worked in a cold, dark room, spending entire days bent over looms. These teens served as bonded laborers, or slaves working to pay off their parents' debts. They worked day and night for no money, and they rarely got to leave the factory.

This incident happened three years after the Nepali government made bonded labor illegal. Since 2000, the country has sent investigators into factories like this one to make sure laws are being followed. These investigators are working to eliminate child labor abuses. In recent years, the government has passed other laws to protect young workers. Today teens between the ages of 14 and 16 can only work six hours a day, and they must receive a minimum wage of 1,420 rupees (U.S.$22) a month.

Carpet weaving also leads to health problems. Because laborers work long hours in dark, dusty conditions, they tend to suffer from eyestrain, headaches, and lung problems. These teens spend hour upon hour knotting wool or weaving thread. They often end up with hand problems such as arthritis.

Parttime Work

Urban teens who attend school are more likely to work in the service industry. Some teens take to the streets before or after school to work as vendors. They sell products such as cigarettes, soft drinks, and newspapers to passersby. Others leave their home in the morning with towel and wax in hand to earn a living by polishing shoes. Teens may work in restaurants as waiters, waitresses, dishwashers, and cooks. Others work behind the counter at clothing stores, markets, or hotels.

Crushing rocks is a common after-school job for rural teens. Young people search the countryside for rocks and then spend hours crushing them into gravel by hand. They then sell the gravel to companies that use it to build roads and trails. Like factory work, rock crushing takes its toll on a teen's health, often resulting in joint problems and illnesses. But the work can earn 100 to 300 rupees (U.S.$1.55–$4.65) a day.

Higher Education

In the past, the few Nepali teens lucky enough to seek a college degree had to

More than 10,000 teens and younger children are thought to work in rock quarries.

travel out of the country to attend universities elsewhere, such as in India, the United Kingdom, or the United States. While nearly 8,000 Nepali teens still choose to study abroad every year, around 140,000 students opt to attend universities in their homeland. Nearly 500 institutions of higher education span the mountainous nation, offering higher education to Nepali teens who can afford it.

Nepal has five major universities, and nearly every other college in the country is somehow affiliated with one of these five. For instance, the government-run Tribhuvan University, Nepal's oldest and largest university, has a main campus outside Kathmandu in the city of Kirtipur. However, a student does not have to live in Kirtipur to earn a degree from Tribhuvan University. The university has 283 affiliated campuses spread throughout Nepal. These campuses give rural teens the opportunity to earn a college degree. Students enrolled on the main campus have access to modern facilities, including the largest library in the country, sports fields, and a medical teaching hospital. The affiliated campuses tend to be smaller and have fewer facilities.

At universities like Tribhuvan, students can choose almost any major offered at Western universities, including agriculture, management, medicine, forestry, technology, education, and engineering. Students can earn intermediate degrees, bachelor's degrees, master's degrees, and doctoral degrees.

The most popular college major in Nepal is medicine. A high percentage of teens hope to be doctors, nurses, pharmacists, or veterinarians. This is not surprising, considering that almost every region of Nepal, except Kathmandu Valley, suffers from inadequate medical care. Other popular

Training at Home

Some teenagers learn labor skills at home. For hundreds of years, certain ethnic groups in Nepal have made their living through a particular trade. Today those skills are still taught to the younger generation. Teens in rural areas especially may learn their future occupation from their parents and grandparents. Some examples:

- The Sherpas, many of whom live in the Mount Everest region, work as mountain guides and porters. Taught by their parents, teen Sherpas guide tourists up and down the tallest peak in the world.
- The Majhi group has made its living on Nepal's rivers for hundreds of years. Many teens learn fishing and boating from their parents at a young age.

There are an estimated 20,000 to 30,000 child laborers in Kathmandu alone, and more than 5,000 homeless children throughout Nepal. While receiving national attention, the number of child laborers has not decreased, primarily because of the country's poor economy.

career routes include government, education, and industry.

Where's My Job?

Male and female teens say that their greatest fear is not finding a job after college. The country's unemployment rate is 42 percent, and young graduates make up a large portion of this group. Graduates have a difficult time finding professional and managerial jobs.

The insufficient job market leads many teens to find work in other countries. An estimated 1.2 million Nepalis work in 40 countries, including India, Malaysia, South Korea, the United States, and various Middle Eastern countries. These workers, including teens, usually send money back to their families in Nepal. Many families rely on this income to survive.

As the nation develops and modernizes, it needs more workers to do skilled manual labor jobs. To fill this need, the country has begun to build more vocational schools. At these institutions, teens train to enter fields such as carpentry, plumbing, and mechanics. Currently the number of vocational schools is small, but teens are beginning to see the value of such an education: It is more likely to lead to employment.

How Nepali teens spend their free time has a lot to do with where they live.

6

Playing Hard

IN GENERAL, NEPALI TEENS HAVE LESS TIME FOR FUN AND FRIENDS THAN TEENS IN MORE DEVELOPED COUNTRIES. When they do have free time, they try to make the most of it. Teens in urban areas, for instance, may go to the newest Nepali action movie, out for pizza, or to the swimming pool. They watch MTV and surf Internet chat rooms. In rural areas, teens may fill their free time with village celebrations, mountain treks, or traditional sports such as *dandi biyo*, a game played with sticks. Nepali teens try to pack their free time with fun, friends, and relaxation.

Rivers and Peaks

Nepal boasts a number of rivers, lakes, and streams that can provide an afternoon of relaxation or adventure for teens. Swimming in some of the rural waterways is out of the question because people use them as bathrooms. Rivers in many parts of the country that were at one time considered sacred are now being drained for factories and

dandi biyo
dan-dee bee-yo

Dandi Biyo

Dandi biyo is a traditional game that has been played by teens and young children in Nepal for centuries. Today the sport is generally played by young people in rural areas. One reason this game has remained popular is that it is cheap and easy—you just need two sticks. Teens compete by hitting the biyo (a little stick) with the dandi (a bigger stick), sending the biyo soaring through the air. Players receive points based on how far they hit the biyo.

In 2007 the Nepal Dandi Biyo Association was formed. The group's goals are to find and unite dandi biyo clubs, standardize the game, and create written rules for tournaments and other competitions. Bijay Poudel, the founder of the group, said:

It's not easy, because we are in an initial stage. But if all those concerned give enough attention to the game we loved to play, then it's not that difficult either.

household use, while others are being used as garbage dumping grounds.

A Nepali resident who lives near the Bagmati River said:

When I was a child we used to swim in the river, but right now it's like a sewer. I cannot believe that. It's a national tragedy because this is our holy river.

But families still come to the water's edge to enjoy an afternoon picnic or, if the water looks clean, an evening swim.

More recently, Nepal's rivers have become popular places for friends, families, and tourists to go whitewater rafting. Groups take to the river for a wild ride through rapids and whirlpools. Rafting is just one of the many tourist attractions for adventure seekers in Nepal. More than 375,000 tourists from across the globe visited Nepal in 2006. Tourism is big business, accounting for 2 percent to 4 percent of the country's gross domestic product.

The mountains provide another recreational setting. In Nepal, mountain fun does not mean skiing, snowboarding, or tubing, as it might in other countries. Instead, teens living in the mountain and hill regions are more likely to spend their free time exploring trails and trekking along mountain passes. Walking or biking with friends along these trails allows them the opportunity to encounter some of the most beautiful scenery and rarest wildlife in the world. Bike riders on Himalayan trails, for instance, may hear the unique call

of the Himalayan snow cock, see a yak, or maybe even come across the elusive snow leopard.

Though it is much more popular for tourists than local residents, mountain climbing does provide adventure and excitement. Teens who would take on such an activity are mainly those who have been raised in the mountains. People such as the Sherpas and the high-altitude pastoralists or those in nomadic communities have been trained in rock climbing most of their lives.

Since Mount Everest was first conquered in 1953, more than 1,500 people from 64 nations have attempted to scale the mountain. But the trip up Everest is not easy. At least 175 people have died trying to get to the top, and many of their corpses remain on the mountain, frozen where they took their last breaths.

Mount Everest brings much-needed revenue to the government of Nepal. Each team of seven climbers attempting to reach the summit must pay a fee of more than 4.5 million rupees (U.S.$70,000). And each spring, an average of 12 teams attempt the climb. There has been talk of limiting the number of teams allowed each year, but the Sherpa people, who earn their

Nepal
Topographical
map

INDIA

CHINA

H

Karnali River

I

M

A

L

Annapurna

•Pokhara

A

CHINA

Mt. Everest

Lhotse

Mahabharat Range

Y

A

Kanchenjunga

Tarai Plain

Narayani R.

⊛ Kathmandu

Kathmandu Valley

INDIA

Sun Kosi River

Mahabharat Range

Tamur R.

INDIA

•Birganj

Tarai Plain

•Dharan

•Biratnagar

N
W ⊹ E
S

0   25   50 mi.
0   25   50 km

living accompanying the climbers, are opposed. A Sherpa guide to Everest said:

> There are thousands of people in the region who solely depend on the trekkers and mountaineers for their income. If they don't come, these people and their families will starve.

Rural Fun with Friends

Rural Nepali teens make weekend plans with friends and try to spend at least a little time away from their parents. In a region without movie theaters, dance parties, or restaurants, though, and where few people have access to television or the Internet, teens have to be creative when it comes to filling their free time. Various ethnic groups have their own ways for teens to meet and interact. For instance, Sherpa teens plan and host their own parties, called *changdungs*. These parties offer teens a chance to make friends, chat, and maybe even flirt!

changdungs
chang-doongs

In some hill cultures, teens sing to each other to pass the time. Friends meet in groups or as couples and sing songs about love, friendship, and the beauty of their homeland. As their ancestors did years before, they use singing as a way to flirt with members of the opposite sex. To show a girl how much she means to him, a boy will write and perform a song just for her.

Conquering Everest

Reaching the summit of the tallest mountain on Earth has become the ultimate dream of almost every serious mountain climber. But the people living in the Everest region, mainly the Sherpas, considered the mountain sacred and so originally did not attempt to climb it. Then in the early 20th century, Western climbers began trying to scale the mountain. These climbers would hire local Sherpas to accompany them up the mountain. All attempts to reach the peak were unsuccessful until May 29, 1953, when Edmund Hillary of New Zealand and Tenzing Norgay of Nepal became the first to reach the top.

Some controversy arose afterward when Hillary was knighted by the queen of England but Norgay was not. Other Nepali climbers have claimed that they have received less recognition than British and American climbers, even though Nepalis hold the records for the fastest climbing time, the youngest climber, and the most time spent at the top.

Nepal teens are open to many styles and cultures. It is not uncommon to see teens with Hindu tika on their foreheads wearing Buddhist jewelry and listening to Western music.

Another World in the City

In the city, the frequent festival celebrations often compete with modern forms of entertainment for a teen's attention. City teens shop in stores that sell both traditional Nepali clothing and Westernized brands such as Nike and Adidas. Some even carry cell phones. Though the mountainous terrain sometimes makes reception difficult, in 2005 there were 246,000 cell phone subscribers in Nepal.

City streets, parks, and even ancient Hindu temples are often filled with groups of teenagers. Some groups wear modern Western-style clothing and listen to rap music. Others wear traditional clothing and sing to each other in Nepali. The *topi*, a traditional peaked

topi
toe-pee

hat, covers the heads of traditional young men. Teens may be in groups of all girls, all boys, or a mixture of the two.

Teen groups also meet at shopping malls and movie theaters. Lack of spending money doesn't stop them from window-shopping. Girls are the most common patrons of city shopping centers. They walk through stores, giggling, joking, and looking for the best deals. Thanks to satellite TV and the circulation of American magazines such as *Cosmopolitan*, Western fashion has become popular.

Cell Phones

In February 2005, King Gyanendra, the ruler of Nepal, dismissed his parliament and took complete control of the country. In an attempt to prevent protesters from banding together, he ordered all communication links switched off, leaving the entire country without phone or Internet service—and people unable to contact their families. A student in Kathmandu who was left without service said:

It hasn't been easy adjusting to a lifestyle without SMS [text messaging] and instant information. You're constantly worried about what might be happening back home.

Although Internet and landline service was restored a week later, cell phone service was not turned back on until May. King Gyanendra returned power to parliament in April 2006.

About a third of Nepal's telephone lines are cellular—landlines are difficult to obtain. Some families have waited up to five years for a landline. They are also expensive, costing some families up to 4,000 rupees (U.S.$62) a month, as opposed to cell phone service, which starts at 500 rupees (U.S.$7.75) for six months of prepaid service.

The demand for cellular service has skyrocketed since its introduction in 1999. In 2004, Nepal Telecom, a government-owned company that controls most of the country's cell phone business, announced it had 50,000 cell phone lines available for the public. The next morning, more than 150,000 people stood in line outside stores, hoping to get a phone. In 2005, the company made more than 4.5 million rupees (U.S.$70,000) a day in revenue.

Dating at the Temples

Cell phones and the Internet are heavily used by Nepali teens. Both are used more for socializing and entertainment than finding information.

Dating and open affection may be discouraged in Nepal, but couples still find ways to meet. Recently the courtyards of ancient Hindu temples have become popular places for teens with love interests to rendezvous. Many teens choose to hide their romantic relationships because they don't want to bring shame upon their families. So these teens look for unlikely places to meet. At 1,000-year-old temples devoted to the Hindu gods, they meet under the guise of worship. One teen said these temples provide excellent cover from suspicion:

It's the safest place. And even if we meet our relatives or other friends, they hardly guess the purpose of our being here.

Some cities boast large movie theaters. At these facilities, teens may watch Nepali movies, which tend to be short narratives that include both song and dance. Foreign movies are also popular. Teens in Nepal will wait in long lines to buy tickets for the most recent American or Indian blockbuster.

computers also like to play high-tech computer games by themselves or with groups of friends.

Many teens also enjoy Nepali music, which is as diverse as the country itself. Some singing groups imitate Western rap, hip-hop, and heavy metal bands. Others have a more local flavor. For instance, the genre of *lok pop* has recently become trendy. This style of music combines pop music with the sounds of Nepali folk music. The musicians play traditional instruments such as the *madal*, a two-headed drum, and the *sarangi*, a fiddle. The songs also include echoes that mimic the sounds associated with living in a mountain region.

lok pop
lock-pop
madal
maa-dal
sarangi
sa-rang-ghee

Watching television has become a common pastime in cities and villages with electricity. As recently as 20 years ago, many Nepali teens had never even heard of TV. Today there are 700,000 homes with televisions, and 400,000 of those homes have cable channels. Some families even have access to satellite television, which means they can watch movies and television programs from around the world with a click of the remote. Renting movies on DVD is also popular.

Satellite and cable TV allow teens to watch music video programs, which are by far the most popular television

Fun at Home

Most teens are indoors by 10 P.M., but that does not necessarily mean they are in bed. If they have computers, teens spend evenings on the Internet, writing e-mail and surfing chat rooms. There are 175,000 Internet users in Nepal, most of whom live in cities. Teens with

There are 700,000 homes in Nepal with televisions. Around 400,000 of these have cable access.

programs among teens. They spend hours watching video after video, comparing artists' talents and good looks. Access to MTV has led to the popularity of American artists such as Jennifer Lopez and Jay-Z.

Satellite television is slowly changing the way Nepali teens behave. One student said:

I would not dare to kiss a girl on the road just because they do so on TV, but there have been changes in the way I dress and in the way I look at things.

Sports: Something for Everyone

Another place where the traditional and modern ways collide is sports. Sports have been important in Nepal for centuries, and many participate in the same sports as their ancestors.

Martial arts, such as karate and tae kwon do, are popular sports. Thousands of teens take lessons in schools, at home, or through martial arts classes. Many also participate in tournaments locally and internationally. In fact, young Nepalis won gold medals in tae kwon do and karate during the 2006 South Asian Games.

Volleyball, basketball, cricket, badminton, and soccer are popular as well. Few Nepali boys do not know how to play soccer. Most do not learn the sport at school, though, because few schools in Nepal can afford sports teams. Instead they learn it in parks and in their own backyards from relatives and friends.

Every weekend and after school, groups of boys converge on parks and other flat, open areas to play pickup soccer games. These games are a common way for boys to spend their free time.

In major cities, a few large sporting facilities have been erected. Some of these arenas, such as the Dasarath Rangasala in Kathmandu, can hold more than 20,000 spectators and host national and international soccer competitions several times each year. On weekends, thousands of fans of all ages converge on these facilities to cheer on their favorite teams. Nepali boys tend to be very enthusiastic, and few activities are more exciting for them than watching one of these competitions.

In general, girls receive less encouragement to play or watch sports than their brothers. According to the traditional culture, sports did not fit with a woman's domestic roles. While this belief remains strong today, people are slowly realizing the importance of girls' athletics. Cricket is the most popular sport for girls. In 2003, the country held its first cricket tournament for girls.

Many Nepali boys dream of becoming professional soccer players.

Looking Ahead

NEPAL IS FILLED WITH VARIETY. Teens live in big, glittering cities and small mountain villages. They follow various religions and speak various languages. They play high-tech computer games and make handicrafts, as their ancestors did hundreds of years before. Every year, more teens gain access to television and the Internet. Every year, they continue to perform ancient dances and listen to Nepali folk music. As their country pushes toward development, today's teens must find ways to move their country forward while maintaining the diversity and cultural identity that make it unique.

Nepal's young people are living in a country that is in the midst of major political and social changes. The country moved from a constitutional monarchy to a parliamentary democracy in 2006, so now more groups of people throughout Nepal have a say in their country's present and future than ever before. Where the country goes from here is very much in the hands of its teens. It is up to them to take their people out of poverty while holding on to the diversity, tolerance, and natural beauty that are Nepal.

At a Glance

Official name: Nepal

Capital: Kathmandu

People

Population: 28,901,790 (2007)

Population by age group:
0–14: 38.3%
15–64: 57.9%
65 and over: 3.8%

Life expectancy at birth: 60.56 years

Common languages:
Nepali, Maithali, Bhojpuri, Tharu (Dagaura/Rana),
Tamang, Newar, Magar, Awadhi, English

Religions:
Hindu: 80.6%
Buddhist: 10.7%
Muslim: 4.2%
Kirant: 3.6%
Other: 0.9%

Legal ages:
Alcohol consumption: 21
Driver's license: 16
Employment: 14 in agriculture, 16 in industry
Marriage: 16 (with consent), 18 without
Military service: 18
Voting: 18

Government

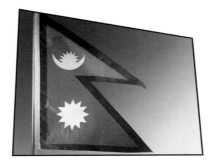

Type of government: Parliamentary democracy

Chief of state and head of government: Prime minister

Lawmaking body: The government of Nepal is in a transition phase; an interim parliament, formed on January 15, 2007, makes laws under an interim constitution.

Administrative divisions: 14 zones, 75 districts

Unification: Under Prithvi Narayan Shah, king of Gorkha, in 1768

Flag: Two-peaked banner, with the peaks representing the country's mountains. Peaks are red with a blue border. On the top triangle is a white crescent moon and 12-poined star. The larger, lower triangle has a bigger star.

Geography

Total Area: 58,872 square miles (147,181 square kilometers)

Climate: The climate of Nepal varies greatly depending on the region and time of year. Residents of northern Nepal experience cool summers and severe winters, while those in the south see subtropical summers and mild winters.

Highest point: Mount Everest, 29,205 feet (8,850 m)

Lowest point: Kanchan Kalan, 229 feet (70 m)

Major rivers: Kosi, Narayani, Gandaki, Karnali

Major landforms: Himalayas, Middle Hills, Tarai Plain

Economy

Currency: Nepali rupees

Population below poverty line: 31%

Major natural resources: quartz, water, timber, hydropower, lignite, copper, cobalt, iron ore

Major agricultural products: rice, corn, wheat, sugarcane, jute, root crops, milk, water, buffalo meat

Major exports: carpets, clothing, leather goods, jute goods, grain

Major imports: gold, machinery and equipment, petroleum products, fertilizer

Historical Timeline

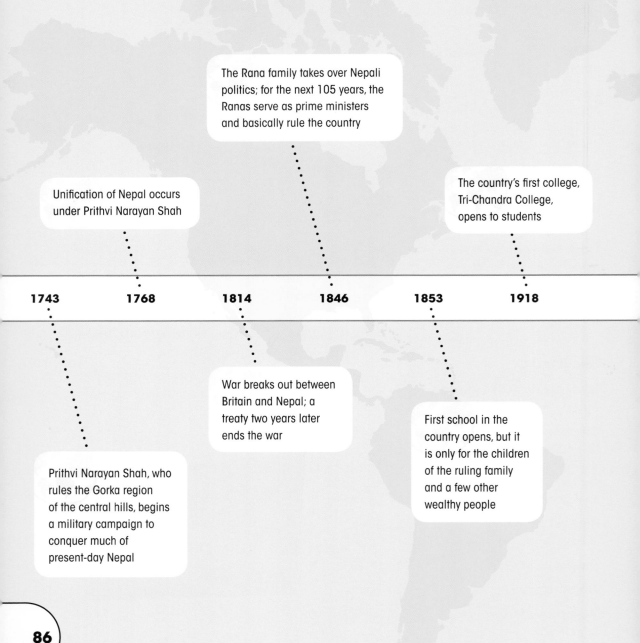

The Rana family takes over Nepali politics; for the next 105 years, the Ranas serve as prime ministers and basically rule the country

Unification of Nepal occurs under Prithvi Narayan Shah

The country's first college, Tri-Chandra College, opens to students

1743   **1768**   **1814**   **1846**   **1853**   **1918**

War breaks out between Britain and Nepal; a treaty two years later ends the war

First school in the country opens, but it is only for the children of the ruling family and a few other wealthy people

Prithvi Narayan Shah, who rules the Gorka region of the central hills, begins a military campaign to conquer much of present-day Nepal

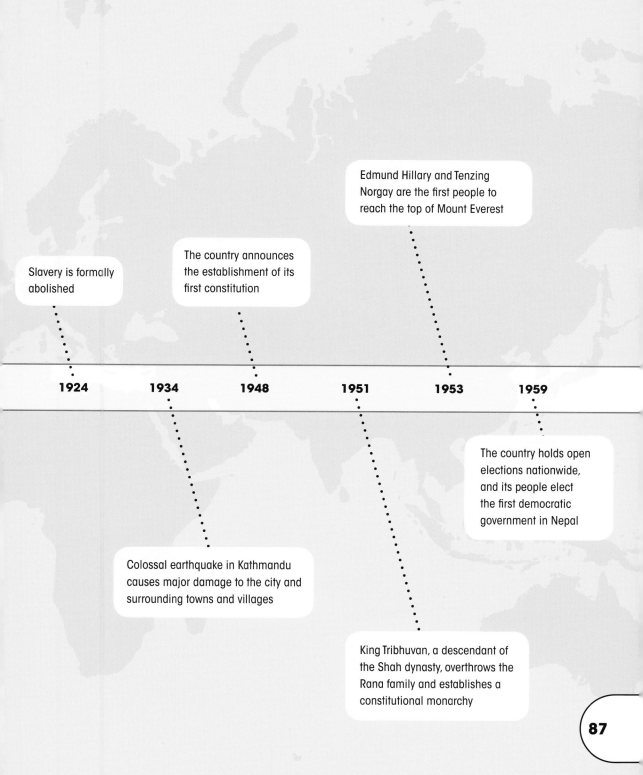

Edmund Hillary and Tenzing Norgay are the first people to reach the top of Mount Everest

The country announces the establishment of its first constitution

Slavery is formally abolished

1924 **1934** **1948** **1951** **1953** **1959**

The country holds open elections nationwide, and its people elect the first democratic government in Nepal

Colossal earthquake in Kathmandu causes major damage to the city and surrounding towns and villages

King Tribhuvan, a descendant of the Shah dynasty, overthrows the Rana family and establishes a constitutional monarchy

Historical Timeline

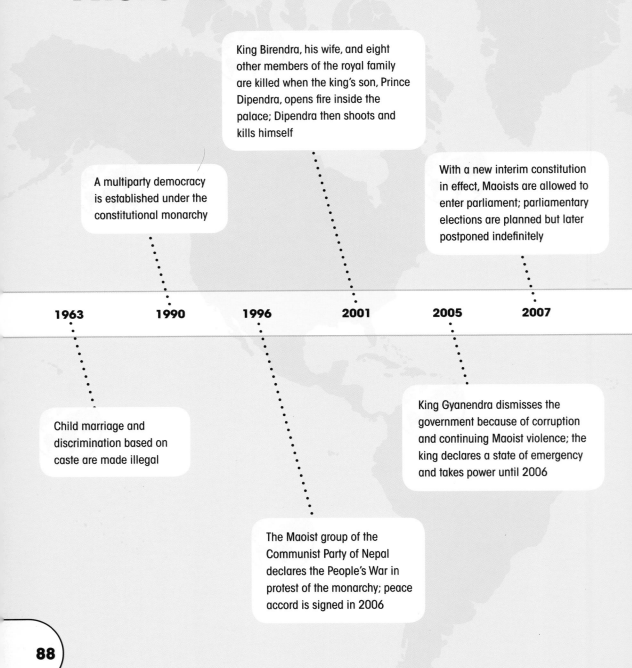

King Birendra, his wife, and eight other members of the royal family are killed when the king's son, Prince Dipendra, opens fire inside the palace; Dipendra then shoots and kills himself

A multiparty democracy is established under the constitutional monarchy

With a new interim constitution in effect, Maoists are allowed to enter parliament; parliamentary elections are planned but later postponed indefinitely

1963   1990   1996   2001   2005   2007

Child marriage and discrimination based on caste are made illegal

King Gyanendra dismisses the government because of corruption and continuing Maoist violence; the king declares a state of emergency and takes power until 2006

The Maoist group of the Communist Party of Nepal declares the People's War in protest of the monarchy; peace accord is signed in 2006

Glossary

Buddhism | major religion founded about 500 B.C. by Buddha, the name given to Siddhartha Gautama by his followers; emphasizes mental and moral purity as a path toward peace and enlightenment

curriculum | courses of study offered at an educational institution

communist | supporter of an economic system in which property is owned by the government or community and profits are shared

Hinduism | world's third largest religion; a central belief is that a person's soul, or spirit, never dies but is reborn in a form affected by the person's thoughts and actions

martial arts | systems of fighting and self-defense, including karate and tae kwon do, that originated in South Asia

nomadic | traveling from place to place according to the seasons in search of food, water, and grazing land

pastoralists | people who raise herds of animals

polygamy | having multiple spouses

polytheistic | believing in more than one god

sari | item of clothing consisting of a long piece of silk or cotton fabric wrapped around the body, with one end draped over the head or one shoulder; often worn by Hindu women

terrain | surface features making up an area of land

vocational schools | schools that prepare students to enter a particular field of employment, usually one that requires skilled workers such as mechanics, plumbers, or carpenters

Additional Resources

FURTHER READING

Fiction and nonfiction titles to further enhance your introduction to teens in Nepal, past and present.

Korman, Gordon. *The Contest.* New York: Scholastic, 2002.

McCormick, Patricia. *Sold.* New York: Hyperion, 2006.

Burbank, Jon. *Nepal.* New York: Marshall Cavendish, 2002.

Miller, Raymond H. *Jhalak Man Tamang: Slave Labor Whistleblower.* Chicago: Thomas Gale, 2006.

Roberts-Davis, Tanya. *We Need to Go to School: Voices from the Rugmark Children.* Toronto: Groundwood Press, 2003.

Werther, Scott P. *Jon Krakauer's Adventure on Mt. Everest.* Danbury, Conn.: Children's Press, 2002.

ON THE WEB

For more information on this topic, use FactHound.
1. Go to www.facthound.com
2. Type in this book ID: 0756534119
3. Click on the Fetch It button.

Look for more Global Connections books.

Teens in Australia	*Teens in France*	*Teens in Mexico*	*Teens in Turkey*
Teens in Brazil	*Teens in Ghana*	*Teens in Morocco*	*Teens in the U.S.A.*
Teens in Canada	*Teens in India*	*Teens in Nigeria*	*Teens in Venezuela*
Teens in China	*Teens in Iran*	*Teens in Russia*	*Teens in Vietnam*
Teens in Egypt	*Teens in Israel*	*Teens in Saudi Arabia*	
Teens in England	*Teens in Japan*	*Teens in South Korea*	
Teens in Finland	*Teens in Kenya*	*Teens in Spain*	

Source Notes

Page 21, column 2, line 7: Katherine Rankin. *The Cultural Politics of Markets: Economic Liberalization and Social Change in Nepal.* Toronto: University of Toronto Press, 2004, p. 122.

Page 44, column 2, line 6: E-mail interview with Rosy.

Page 56, column 2, line 13: E-mail interview with Selena.

Page 59, sidebar, line 2: "Expanded Choices for Adolescents in Nepal." EngenderHealth. 2005. 12 May 2007. www.engenderhealth.org/itf/nepal.html

Page 72, sidebar, line 21: Ujjwal Acharya. "Lofty Dreams for a Little Game." eKantipur.com. 24 January 2007. 19 July 2007. http://kantipuronline.com/kolnews.php?&nid=98521

Page 72, column 2, line 5: Alastair Lawson. "World: South Asia: Nepal's Sacred River Under Threat." BBC News. 21 July 1999. 15 June 2007. http://news.bbc.co.uk/1/hi/world/south_asia/395316.stm

Page 75, column 1, line 3: MountEverest.net. "Summiteers per Climbable Altitude m: Blanc 9.09-Everset.05!" explorersweb. 20 April 2004. 20 July 2007. www.mounteverest.net/story/stories/SummitrsprlimbablaltitudmBlan909-Evrst05Apr182004.shtml

Page 77, sidebar, line 12: "Living Without Cell Phones." Nepal News. *Kathmandu Post.* 7 March 2005. 8 Oct. 2007. www.happy-nomads.nl/nepal-nieuws/cell-phones.html

Page 78, sidebar, line 17: Sangeeta Rijal. "Dating at Temples." Ekantipur.com. 25 June 2004. 19 Jan. 2007. www.kantipuronline.com/kolnews.php?&nid=13582

Page 80, column 1, line 10: David Page and William Crawley. "Satellites Over South Asia: Broadcasting, Culture and the Public Interest." Media South Asia. 2001. 18 Oct. 2007. www.mediasouthasia.org/introduction.asp

Pages 84-85, At a Glance: Nepal. Central Intelligence Agency. *The World Factbook—Nepal.* 18 Oct. 1007. 22 Oct. 2007. https://www.cia.gov/library/publications/the-world-factbook/geos/np.html

Select Bibliography

Asian Development Bank. "Technical Assistance to the Kingdom of Nepal for Restructuring of Nepal Electricity Authority." 2004. 10 Feb. 2006. www.adb.org/Documents/TARs/NEP/tar-nep-37196.pdf

Central Intelligence Agency. *The World Factbook: Nepal.* 18 Oct. 2007. 23 Oct. 2007. https://www.cia.gov/cia/publications/factbook/geos/np.html

Greene, Paul D. "Nepal's *Lok Pop* Music: Representations of the Folk, Tropes of Memory, and Studio Technologies." *Asian Music* 34.1 (2002/2003):43–65.

Jha, Sunil Kumar. *Customs and Etiquette of Nepal.* London: Bravo Ltd., 2007.

Maslak, Mary Ann. *Daughters of the Tharu: Gender, Ethnicity, Religion, and the Education of Nepali Girls.* New York: Taylor and Francis Books, 2003.

Matheson, Clare. "Lightening the Load of Child Miners." *BBC News Online.* 12 June 2006. 1 March 2007. http://newsvote.bbc.co.uk/mpapps/pagetools/print/news.bbc.co.uk/2/hi/business/4070746.stm

Nepal Home Page. 25 Feb. 2007. www.nepalhomepage.com

Nepal. Ministry of Education and Sports. *Education in Nepal, 2003.* 19 Jan. 2007. www.moe.gov.np/admin/res_reports/Education_Nepal.pdf

Nepal. Ministry of Education and Sports. *Education in Nepal, 2003: Four Pillars of Ideal Education: Peace, Tolerance, Good Conduct and Employment.* 2003. 19 Jan. 2007. www.moe.gov.np/admin/res_reports/Education_Nepal_Brochure.pdf

Nepal. Ministry of Education and Sports. *Nepal in Educational Figures 2005.* 25 Jan. 2007. www.moe.gov.np/Educational%20Statistics/download%20pdf/Nepal%20in%20Educational%20Figures,%202005.pdf

Nepal. Ministry of Health and Population. *Adolescent Health and Development in Nepal: Status, Issues, Programmes and Challenges.* 2005. 15 Dec. 2006. www.searo.who.int/LinkFiles/Initiatives_AHD_in_Nepal.pdf

Nepal. "Nepal in Figures 2005." 19 Dec. 2006. www.npc.gov.np/nepal/Nepal_in_figure2005.pdf

Nepal Vista. 2007. 19 Feb. 2007. www.nepalvista.com

Rankin, Katherine. *The Cultural Politics of Markets: Economic Liberalization and Social Change in Nepal*. Toronto: University of Toronto Press, 2004.

Rijal, Sangeeta. "Dating at Temples." Ekantipur.com. 25 June 2004. 19 Jan. 2007. www.kantipuronline.com/kolnews.php?&nid=13582

Shrestha, Nanda R., and Keshav Bhattarai. *Historical Dictionary of Nepal*. Lanham, Md.: Scarecrow Press, 2003.

Stash, Sharon, and Emily Hannum. "Who Goes to School? Educational Stratification by Gender, Caste, and Ethnicity in Nepal." *Comparative Education Review* 45.3 (2001): 354–378.

U.S. Department of State. Bureau of Democracy, Human Rights, and Labor. "Nepal: Country Reports on Human Rights Practices 2005." 8 March 2006. 6 March 2007. www.state.gov/g/drl/rls/hrrpt/2005/61709.htm

U.S. Department of State. Bureau of Democracy, Human Rights, and Labor. "Nepal: International Religious Freedom Report 2004." 15 Sept. 2004. 5 March 2007. www.state.gov/g/drl/rls/irf/2004/35518.htm

Varghese, Santosh. "Child Labor in Nepal: Education Combating Unjust Labor." Youth Advocate Program International Resource Paper. 28 Feb. 2007. www.yapi.org/rpchildlabornepal.pdf

Whelpton, John. *A History of Nepal*. New York: Cambridge University Press, 2005.

Index

About the Author
Nicki Yackley-Franken

Nicki Yackley-Franken recently graduated with a master of arts degree in English from Minnesota State University, Mankato. In addition to being an author, she has worked as a journalist and a composition instructor. Raised in Sioux Center, Iowa, Nicki currently lives in Watertown, South Dakota, and works as a librarian and English instructor at the Lake Area Technical Institute.

About the Content Adviser
Mark Turin, Ph.D.

Our content adviser for *Teens in Nepal*, Mark Turin, is a linguistic anthropologist who speaks Nepali and two of the other minority ethnic languages spoken in the country. His research interests include the politics of language and ethnicity in the Himalayas, Nepali traders and workers in India and Tibet, and journalism. He has taught the Nepali language at the university level. He directs the Digital Himalaya Project (www.digitalhimalaya.com) and splits his time between Europe and Nepal.

border to border · teen to teen · border to border · teen to teen · border to border